JAZZ PIANO SOLOS   VOLUME 34

horace silver

Arranged by Brent Edstrom

contents

ISBN 978-1-4950-0744-6

HAL•LEONARD®
CORPORATION

7777 W. BLUEMOUND RD. P.O. BOX 13819 MILWAUKEE, WI 53213

Visit Hal Leonard Online at
www.halleonard.com

THE CAPE VERDEAN BLUES

Words and Music by
HORACE SILVER

Medium Samba

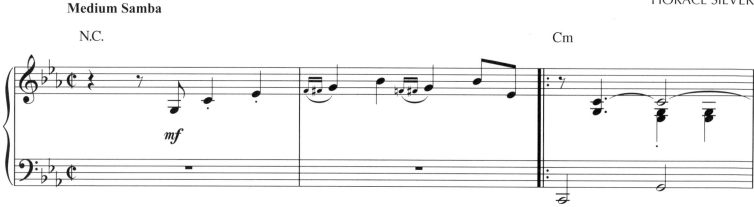

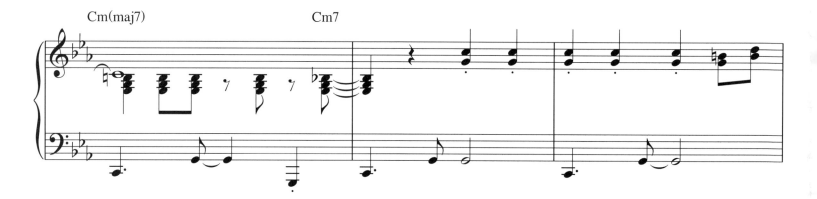

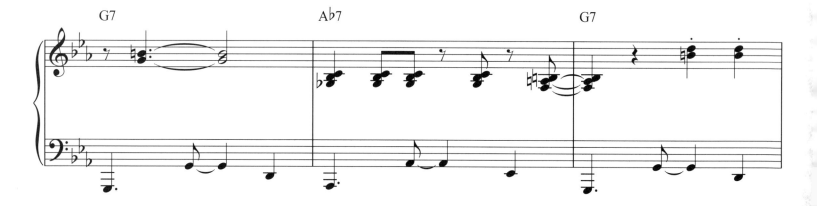

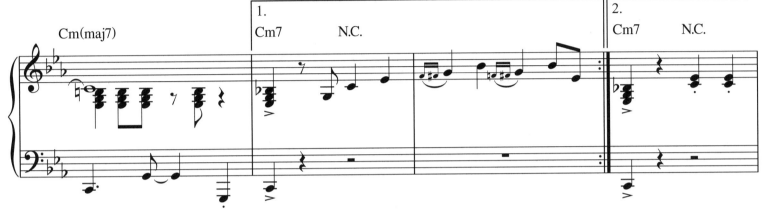

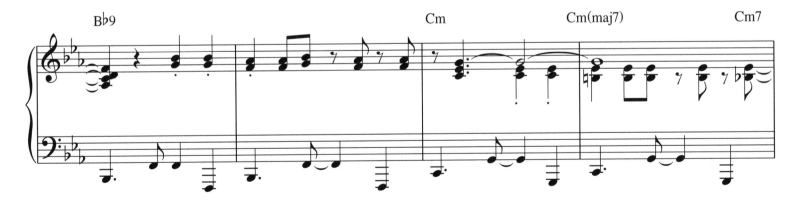

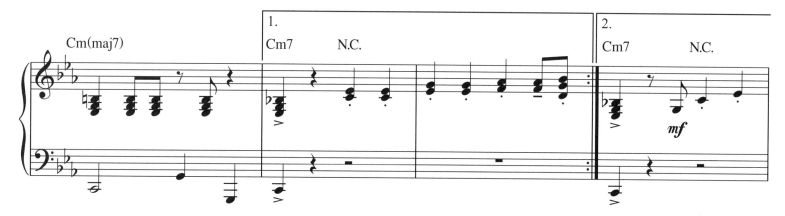

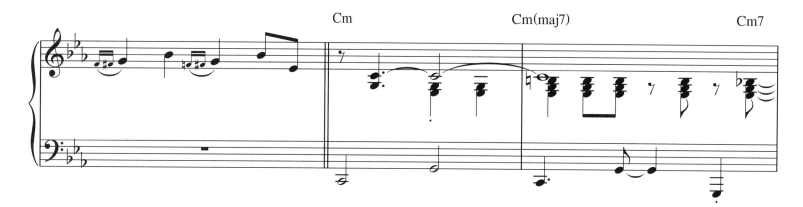

Solo based on one by Horace Silver

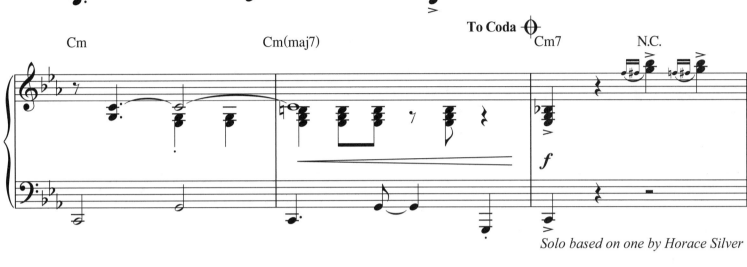

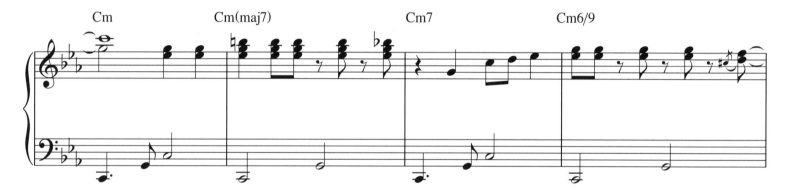

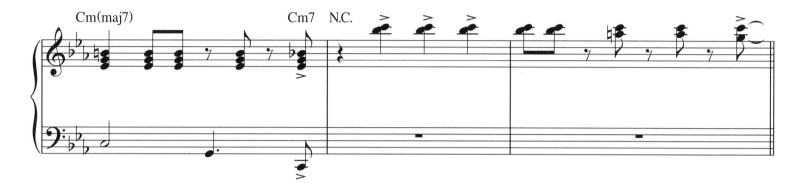

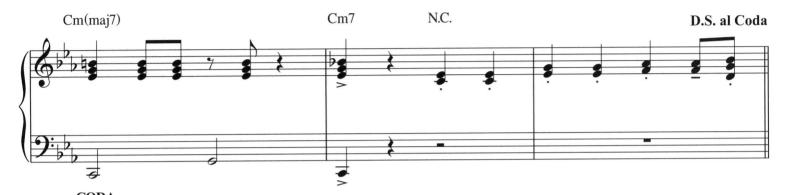

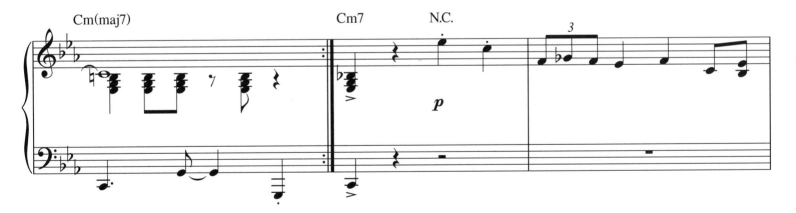

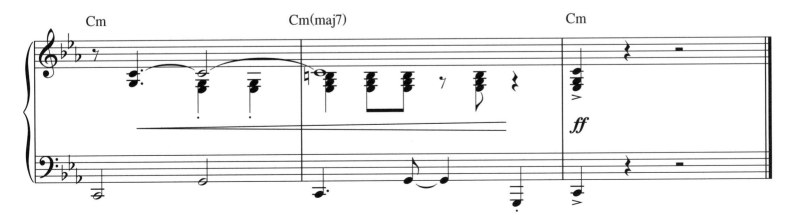

COOL EYES

Words and Music by
HORACE SILVER

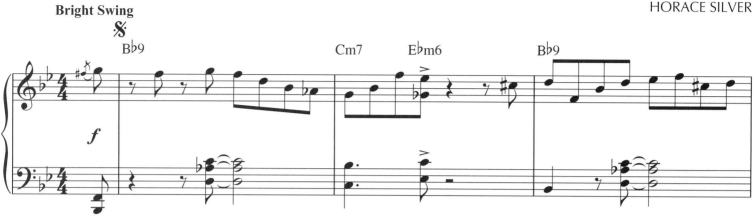

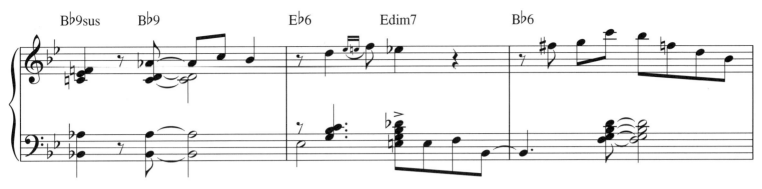

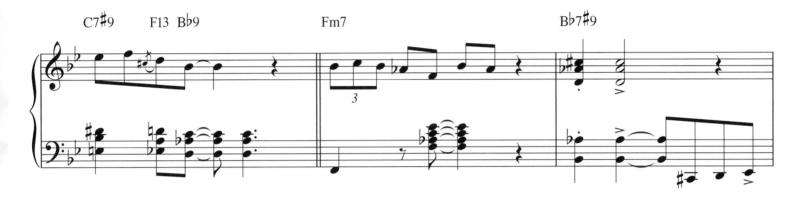

To Coda ⊕

Solo based on one by Horace Silver

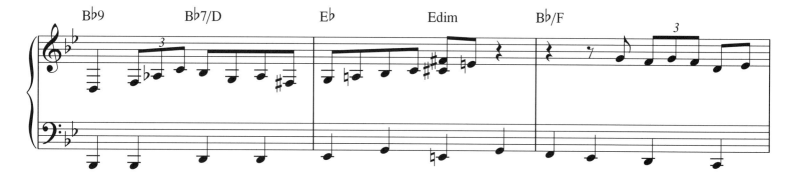

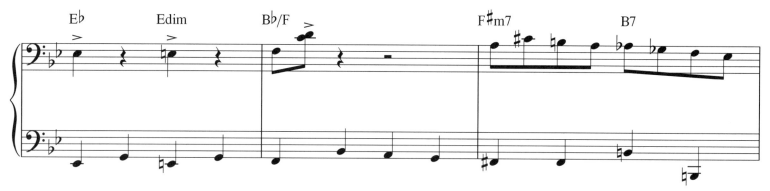

LONELY WOMAN

Words and Music by
HORACE SILVER

Ballad

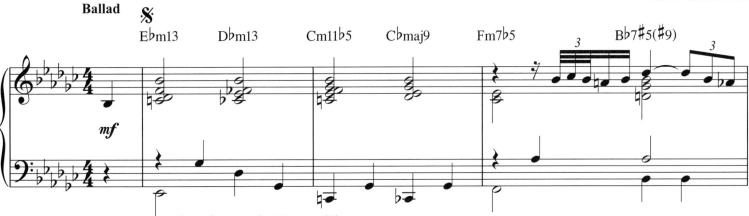

Arrangement based on one by Horace Silver

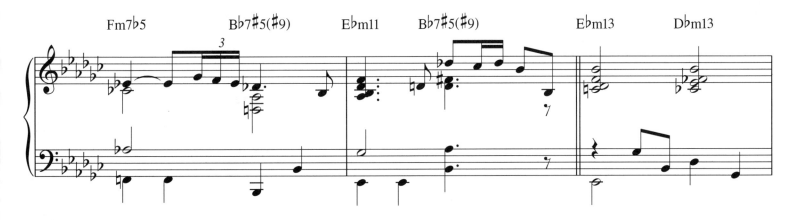

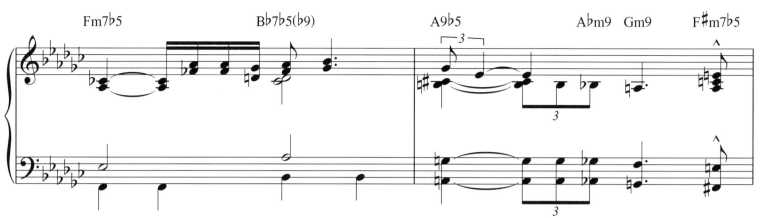

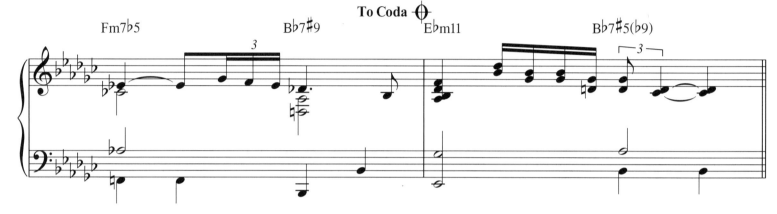

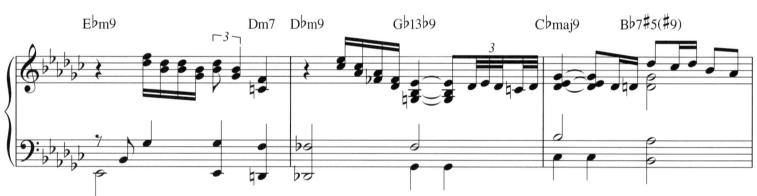

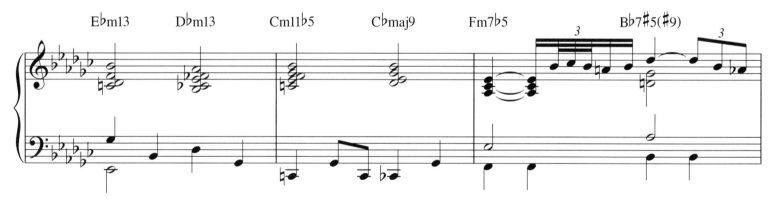

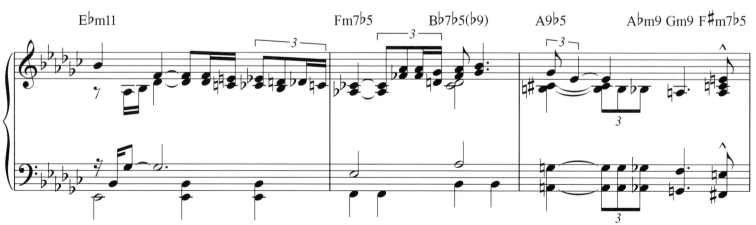

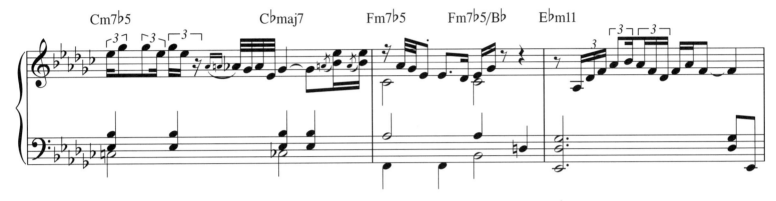

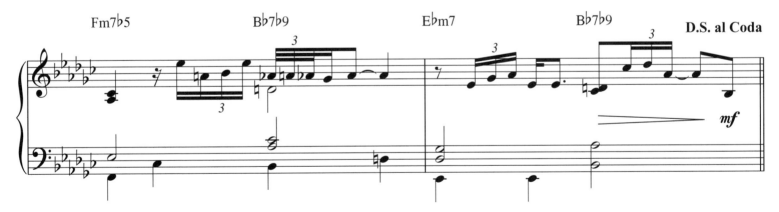

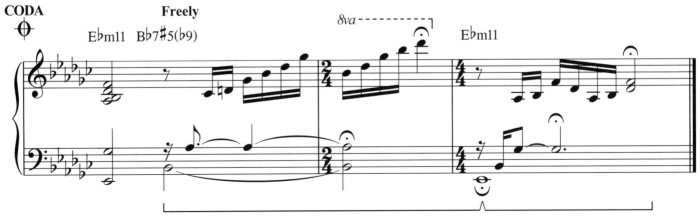

DOODLIN'

By HORACE SILVER

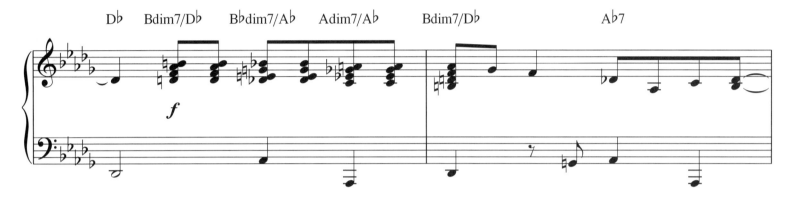

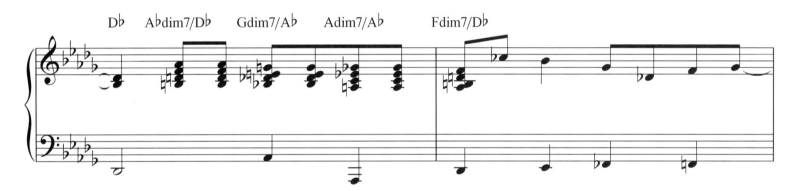

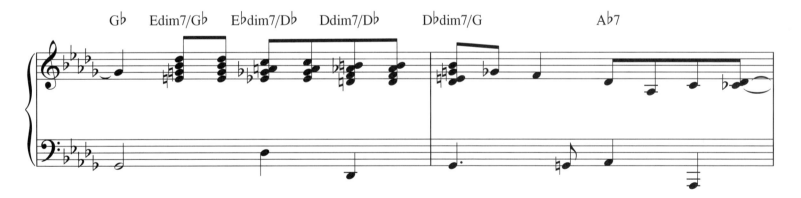

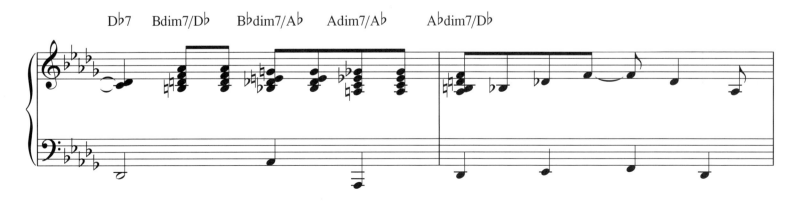

FILTHY McNASTY

Words and Music by
HORACE SILVER

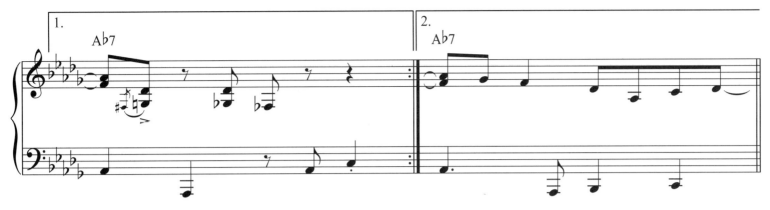

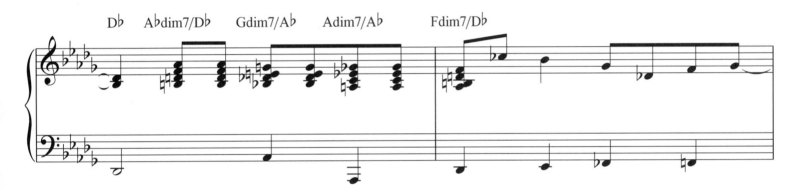

Piano solo based on one by Horace Silver

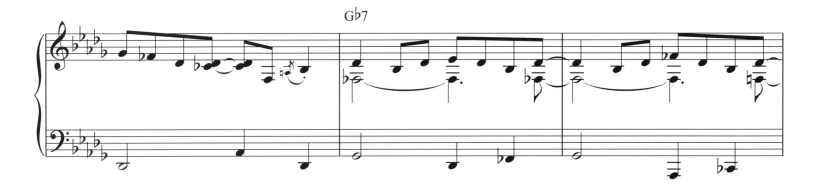

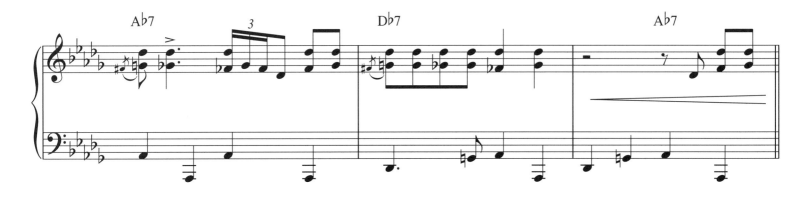

FILTHY McNASTY

Words and Music by
HORACE SILVER

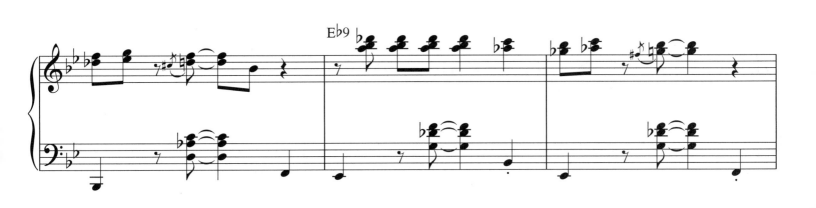

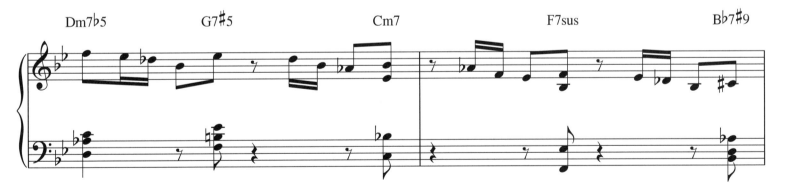

FOR HEAVEN'S SAKE

Words and Music by DON MEYER,
ELISE BRETTON and SHERMAN EDWARDS

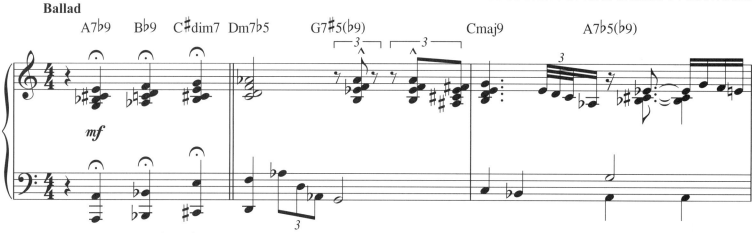

Arrangement based on one by Horace Silver

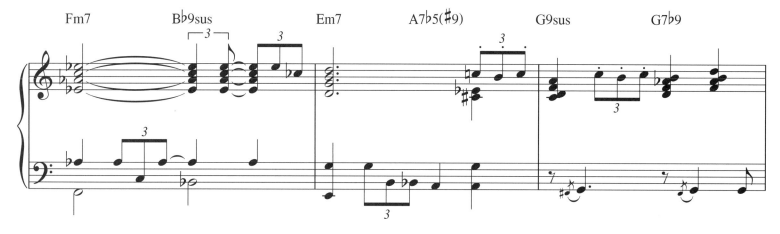

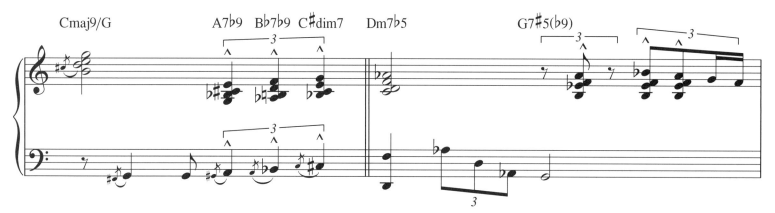

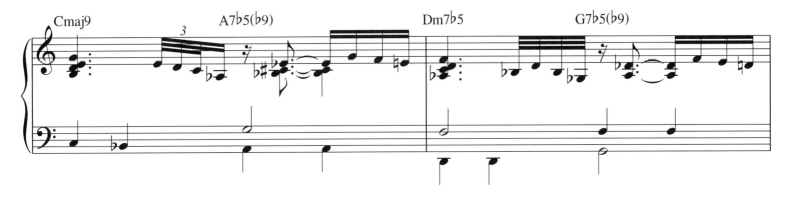

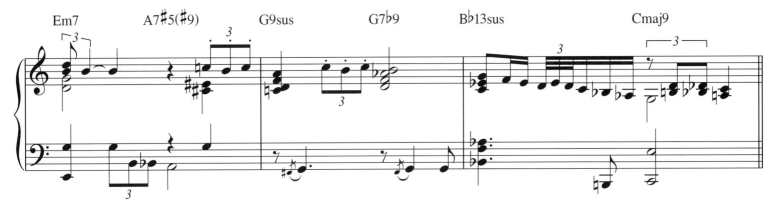

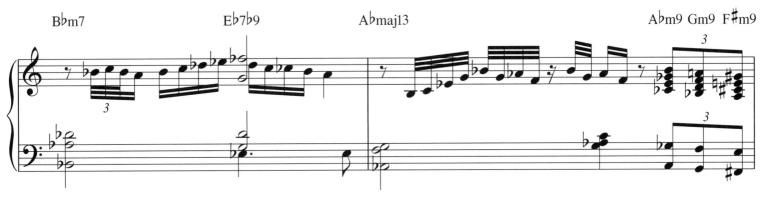

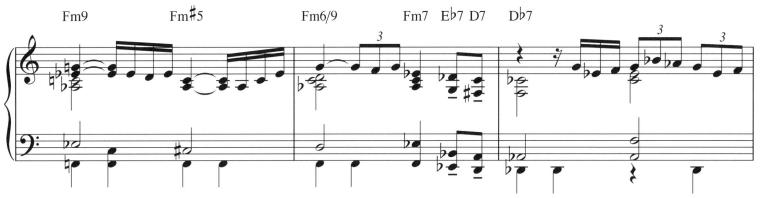

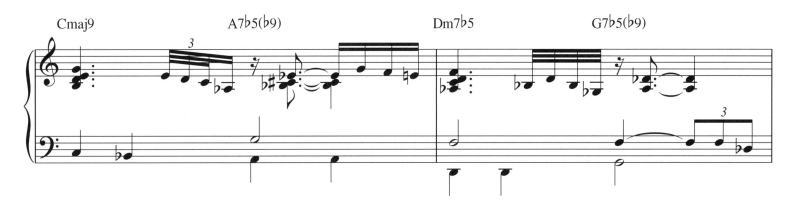

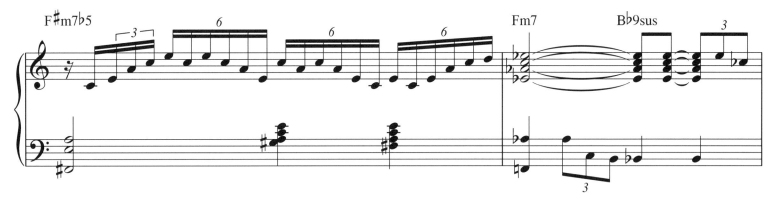

CODA

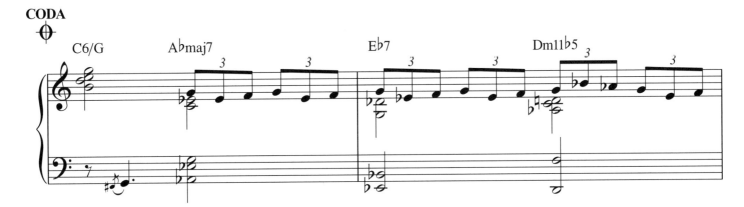

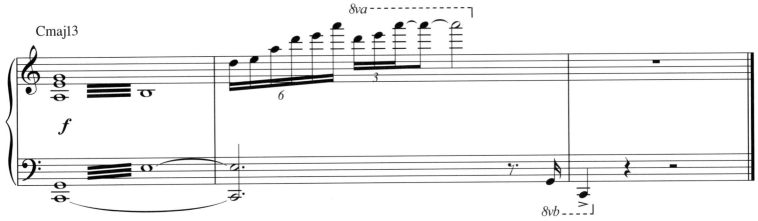

HOW LONG HAS THIS BEEN GOING ON?

from ROSALIE

Music and Lyrics by GEORGE GERSHWIN
and IRA GERSHWIN

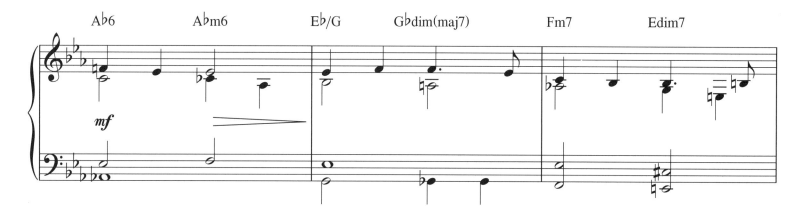

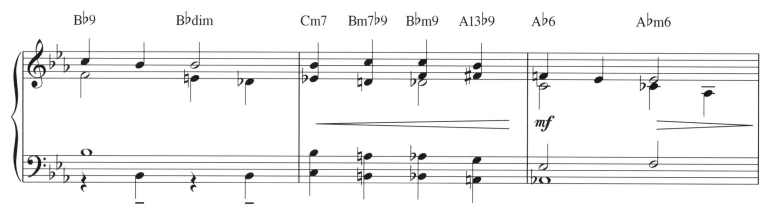

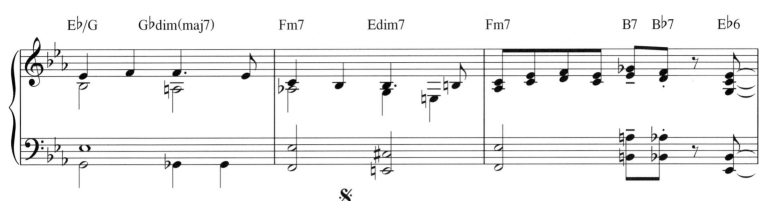

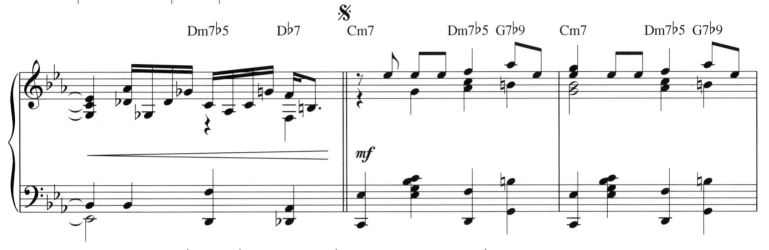

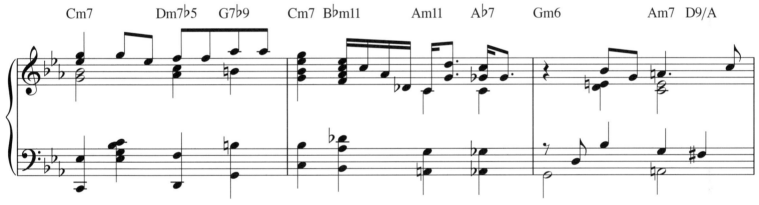

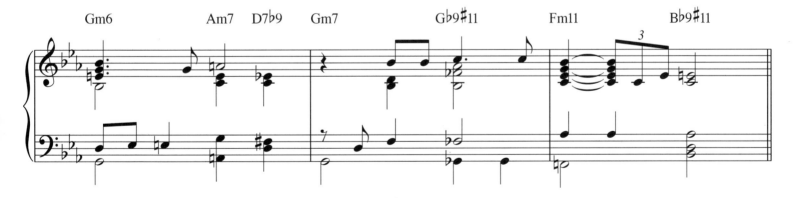

To Coda ⊕

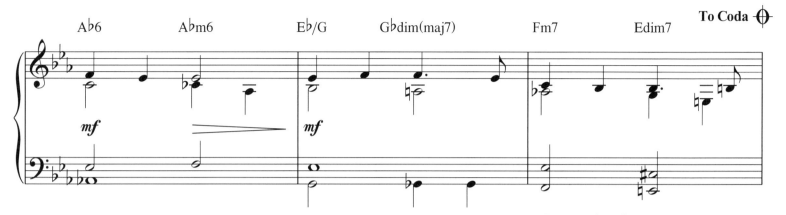

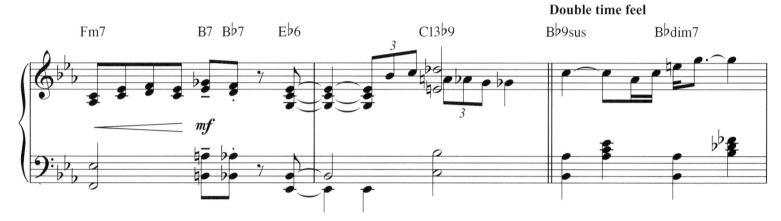

Double time feel

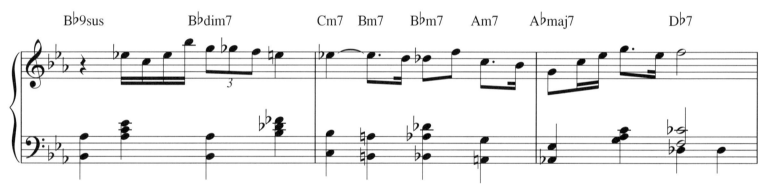

31

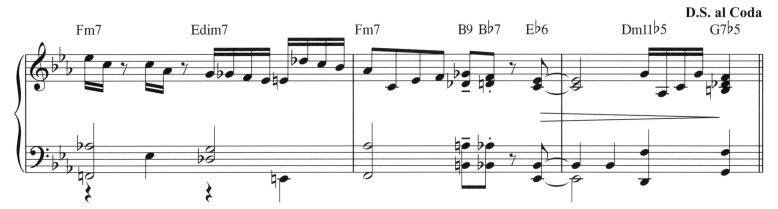

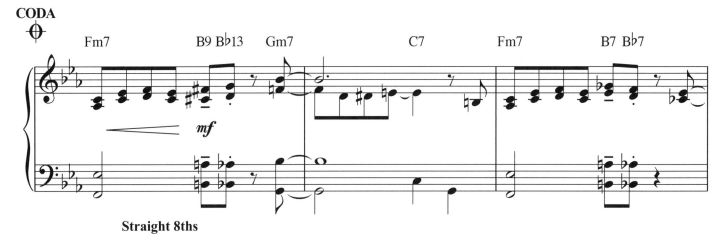

THE JODY GRIND

Words and Music by
HORACE SILVER

Funky Blues

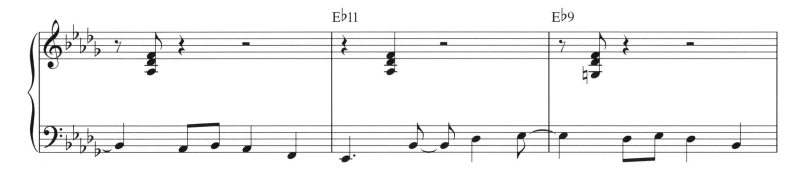

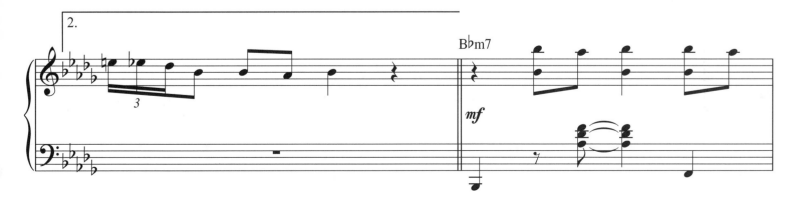

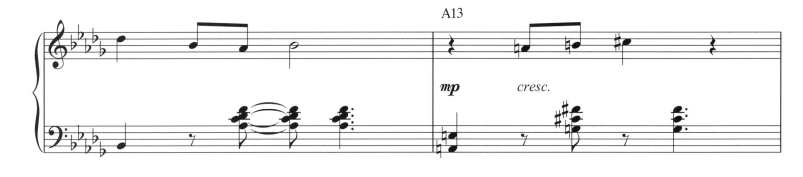

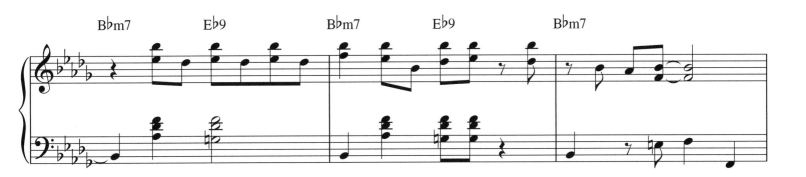

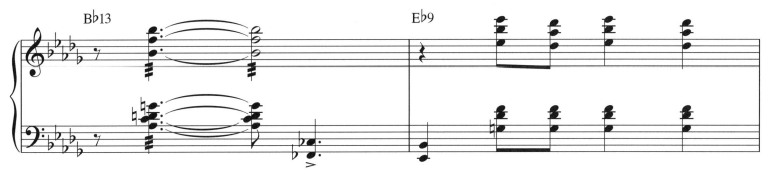

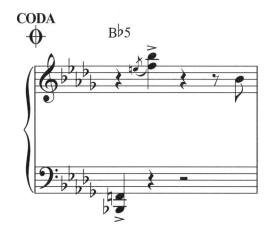

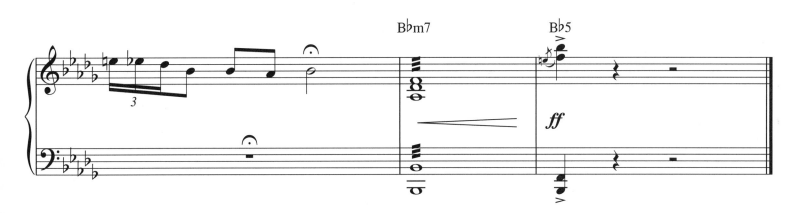

JUICY LUCY

Words and Music by
HORACE SILVER

Medium Swing

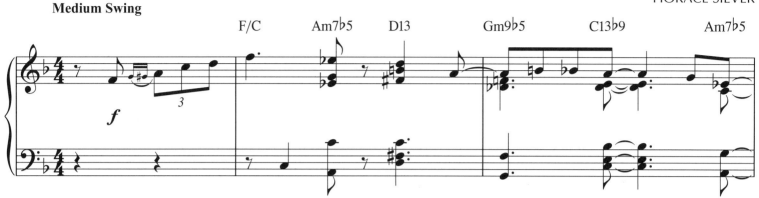

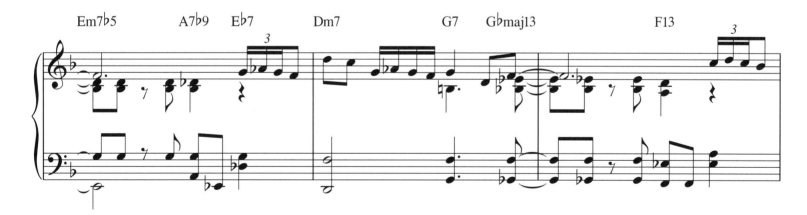

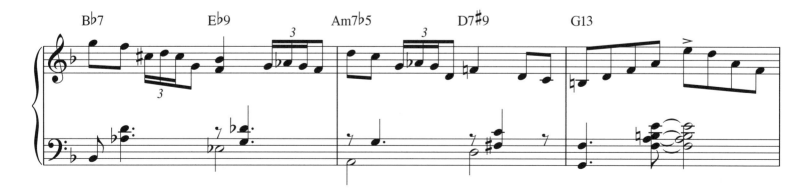

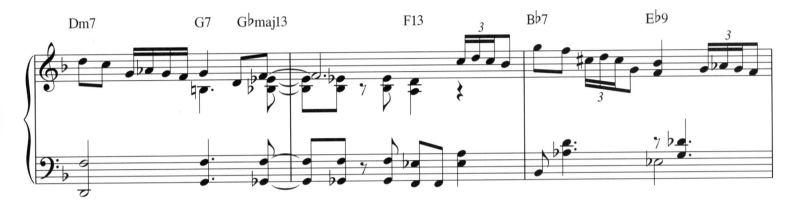

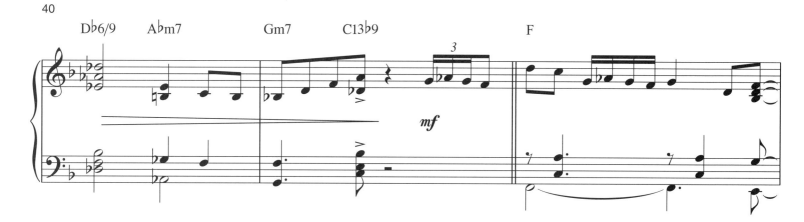

To Coda ⊕

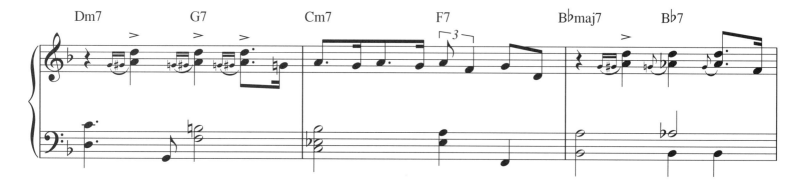

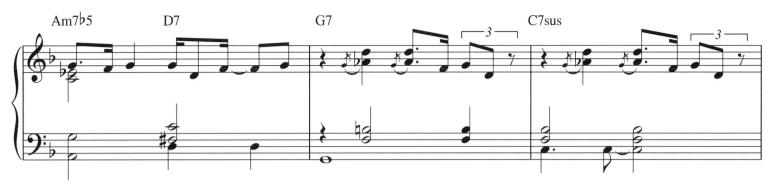

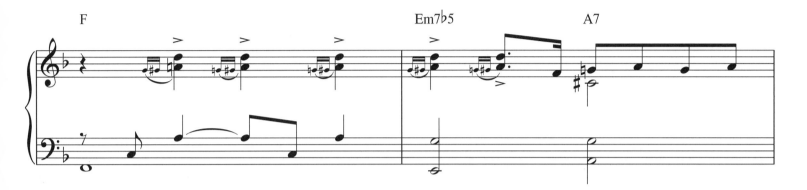

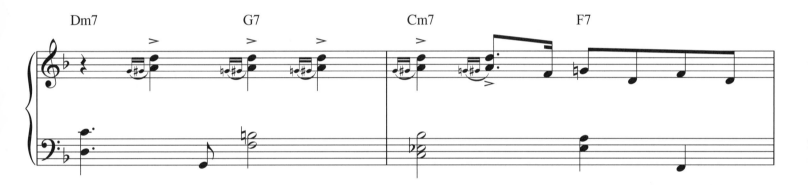

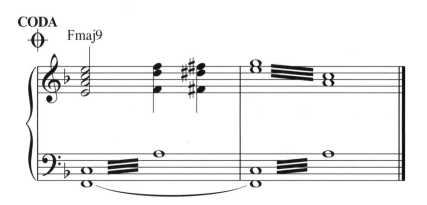

NICA'S DREAM

Words and Music by
HORACE SILVER

Fast Latin

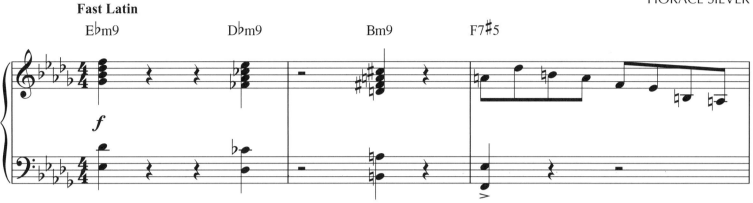

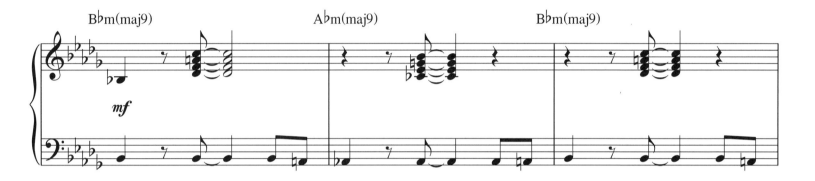

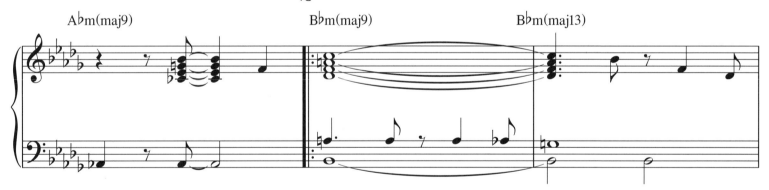

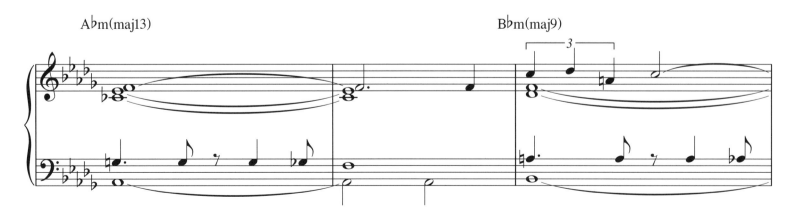

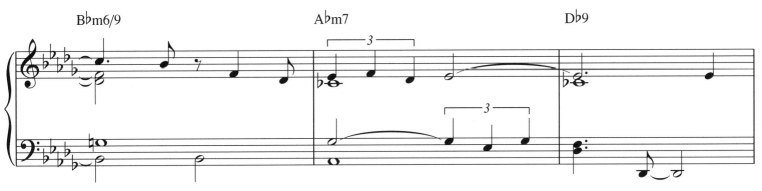

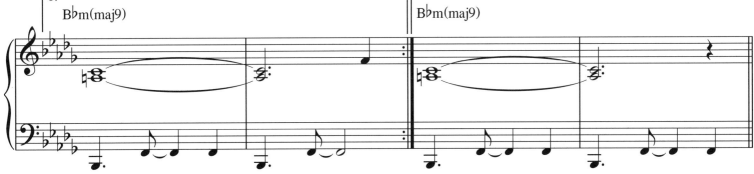

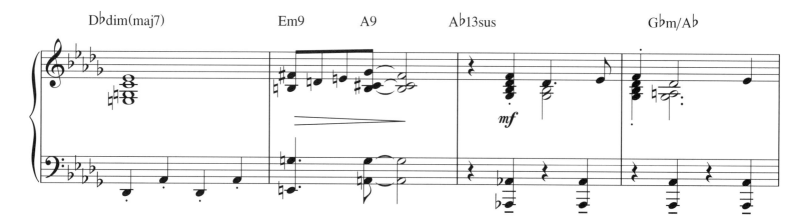

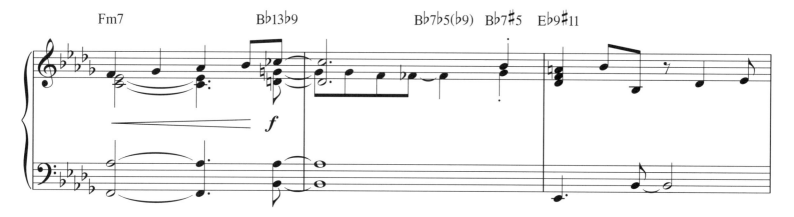

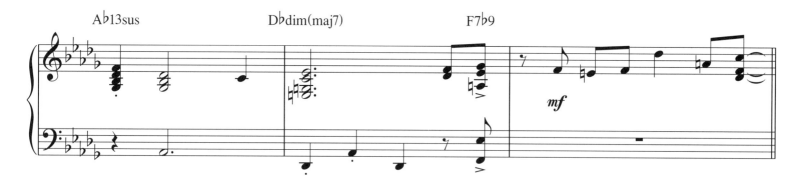

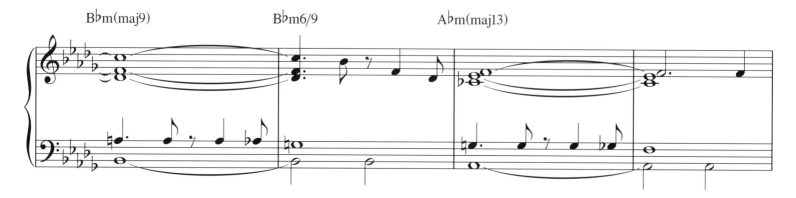

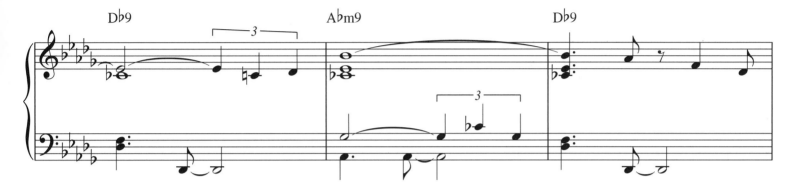

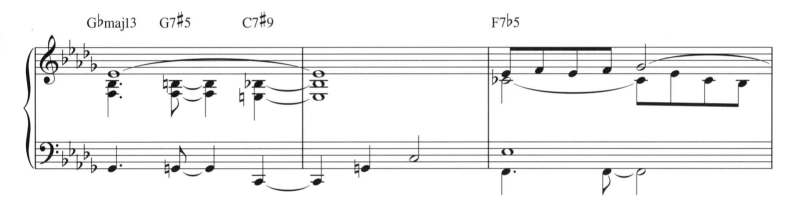

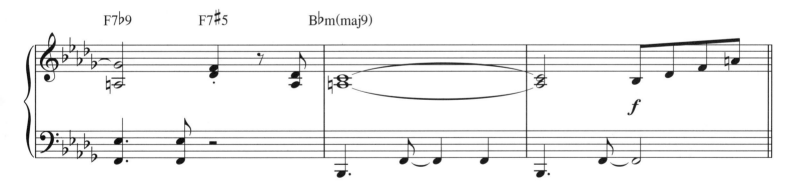

46

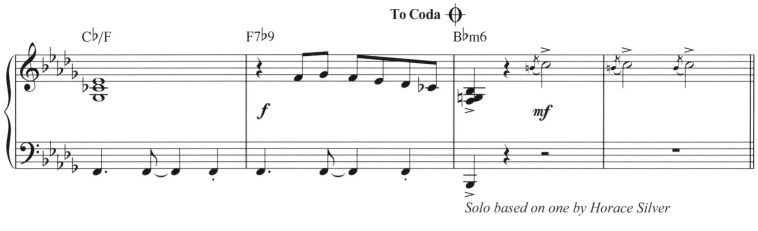

Solo based on one by Horace Silver

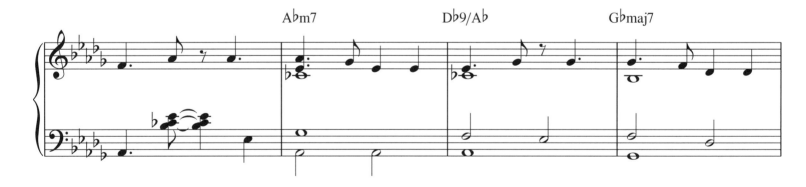

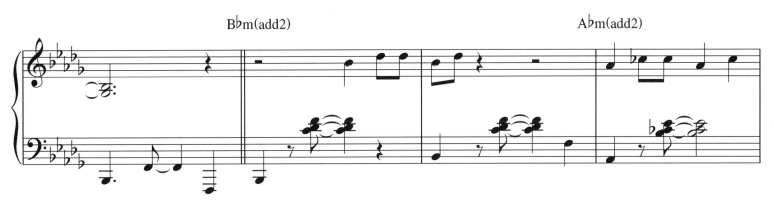

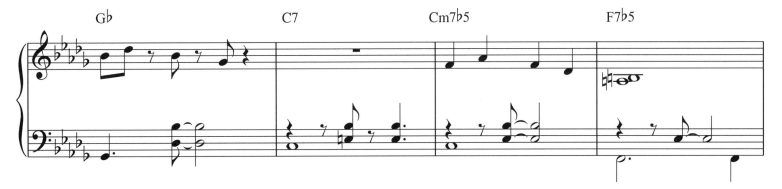

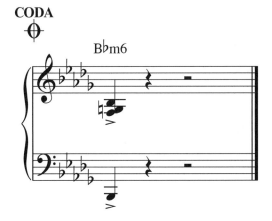

NUTVILLE

By HORACE SILVER

Fast Latin

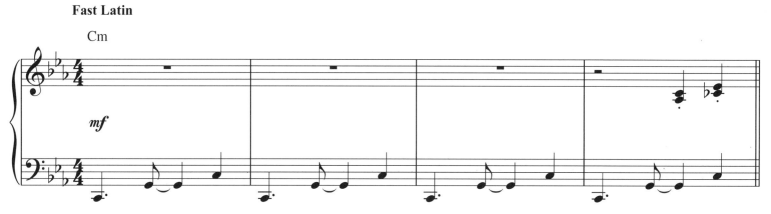

Arrangement based on one by Horace Silver

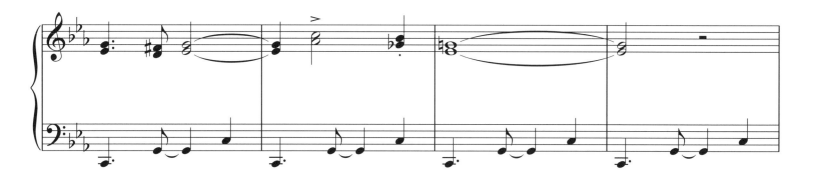

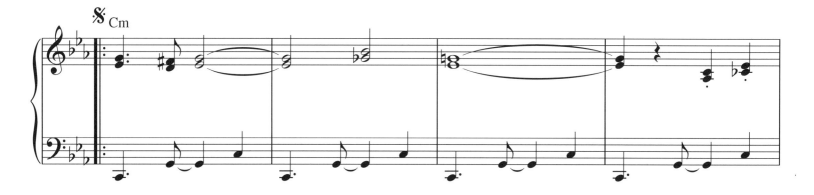

Cm(add2)

Ab13 · G13 · Gb13

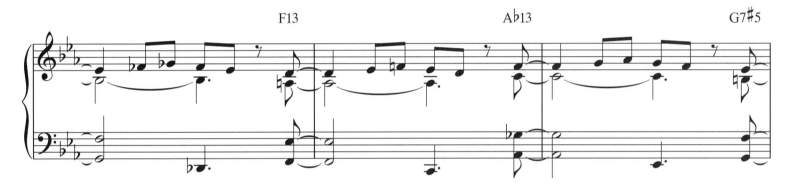

F13 · Ab13 · G7#5

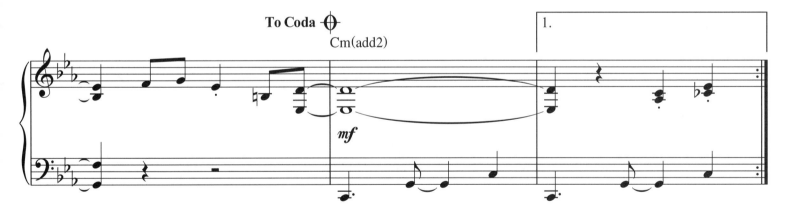

To Coda

Cm(add2)

1.

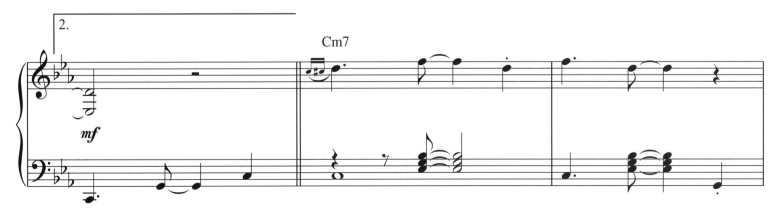

2.

Cm7

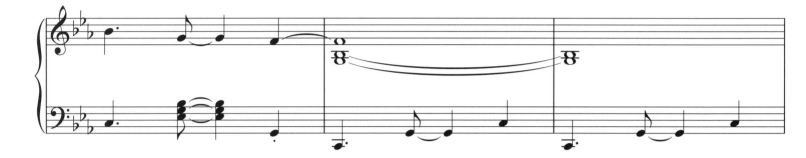

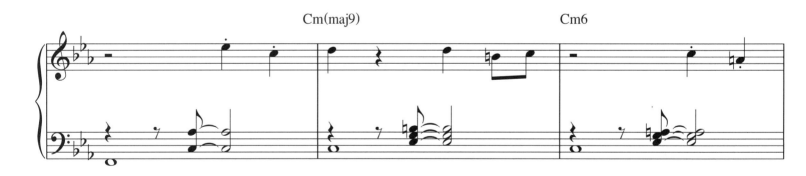

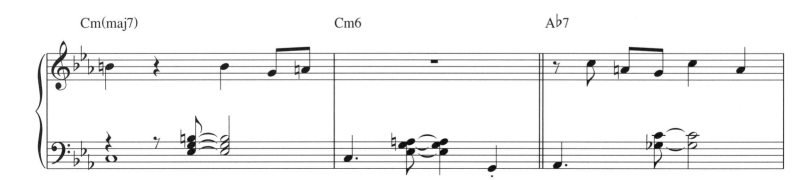

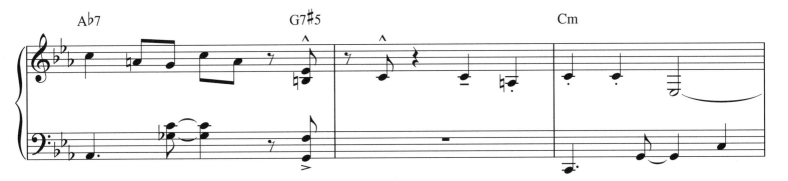

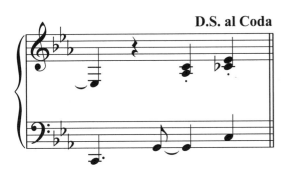

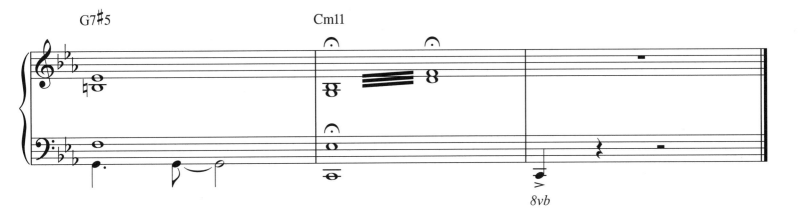

OPUS DE FUNK

Words and Music by
HORACE SILVER

Bop

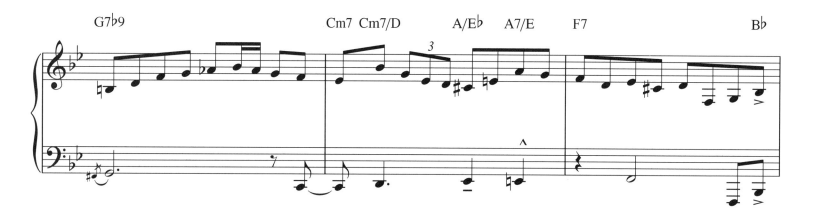

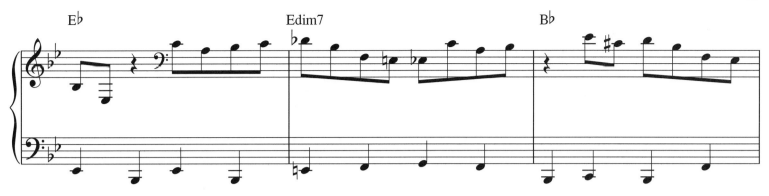

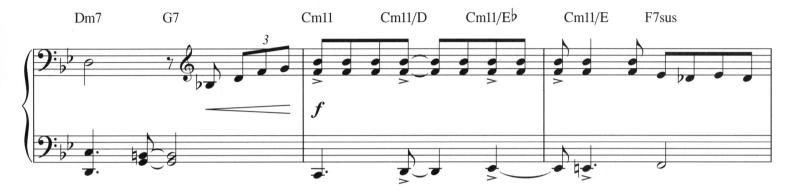

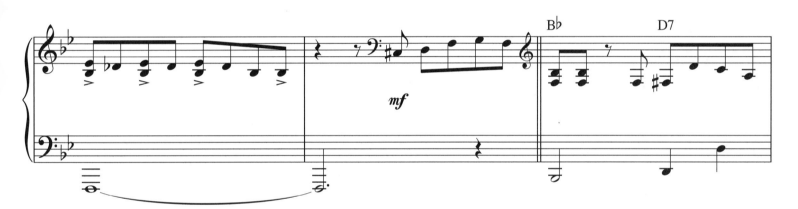

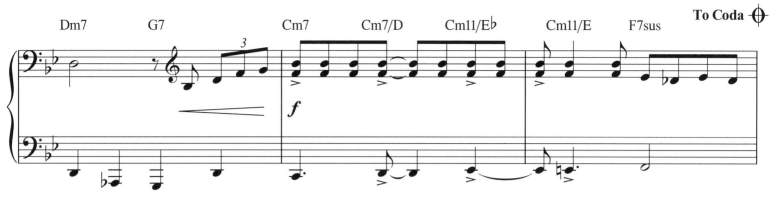

To Coda

Solo based on one by Horace Silver

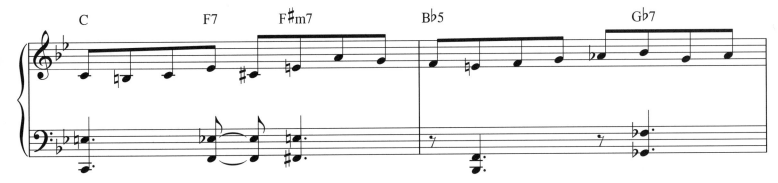

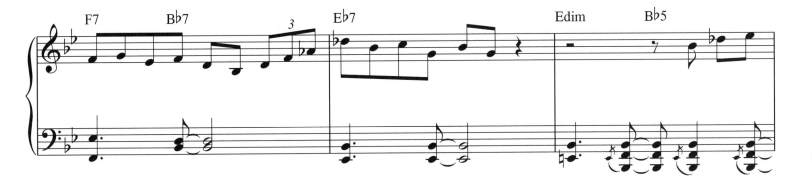

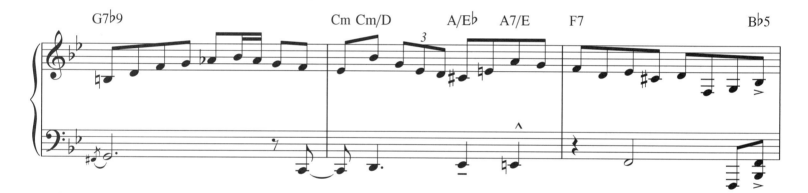

PEACE

Words and Music by
HORACE SILVER

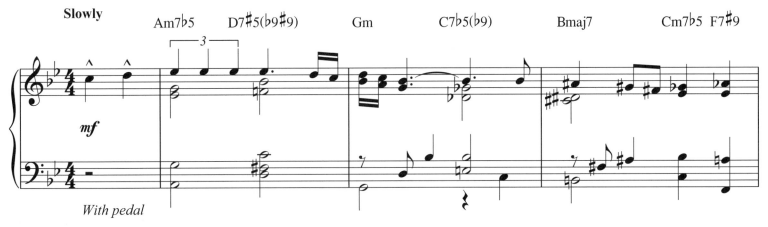

Solo based on one by Horace Silver

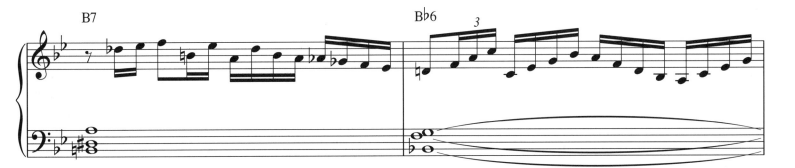

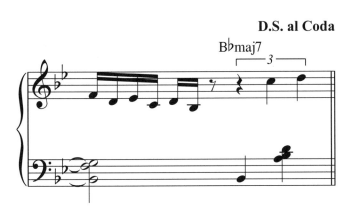

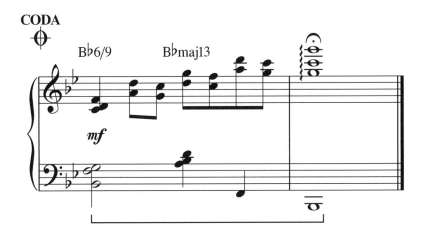

THE PREACHER

By HORACE SILVER

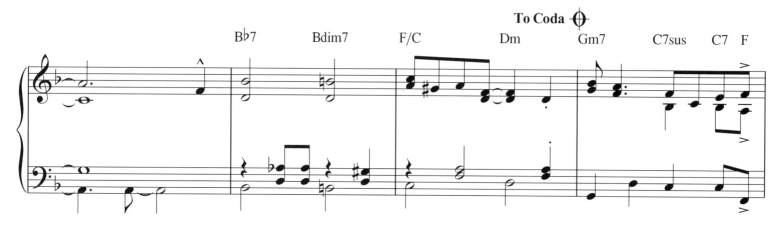

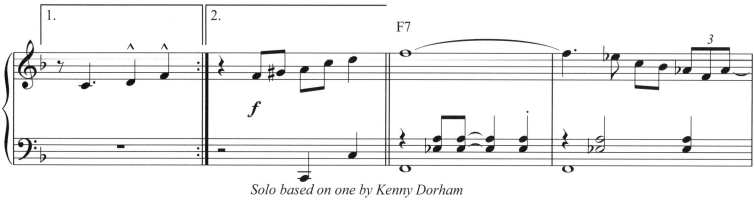

Solo based on one by Kenny Dorham

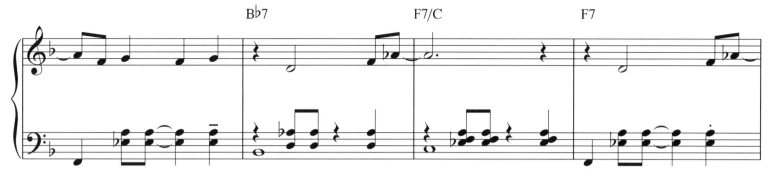

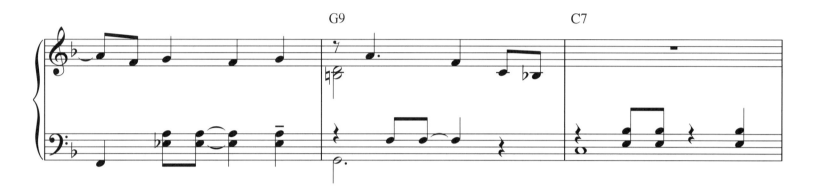

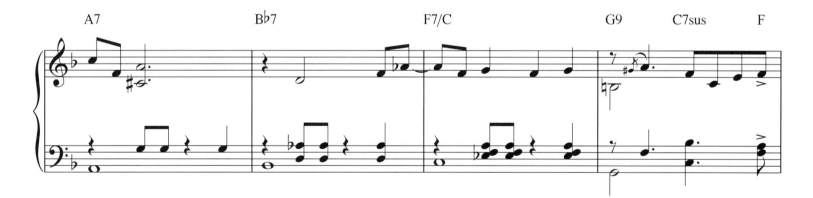

QUE PASA

By HORACE SILVER

Moderately slow Latin groove

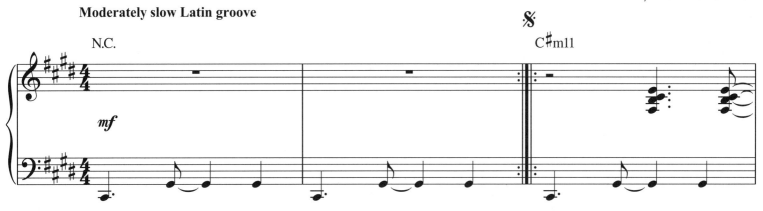

To Coda ⊕

1.

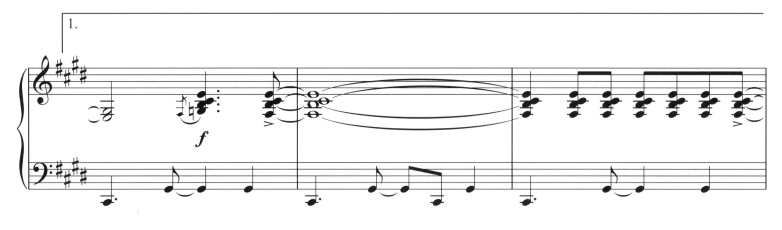

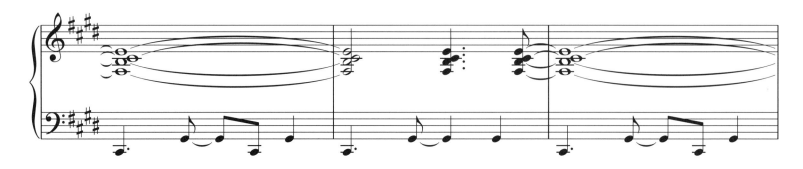

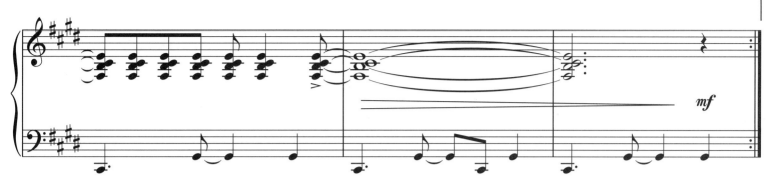

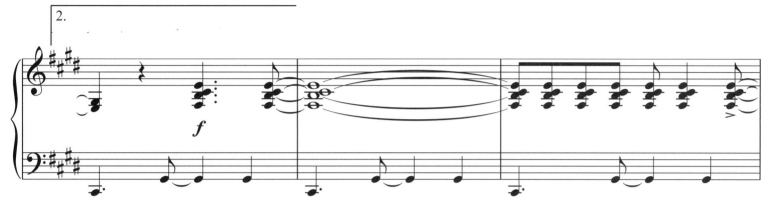

C#m7

C#m11

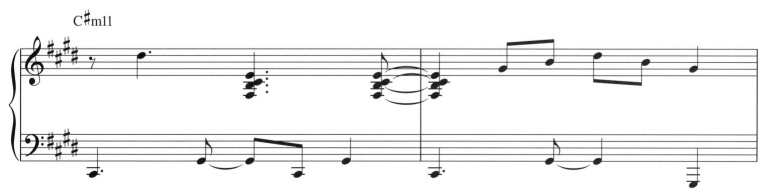

Solo based on one by Horace Silver

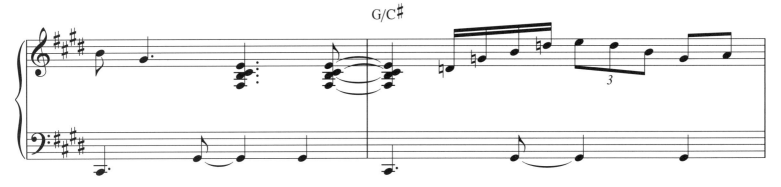

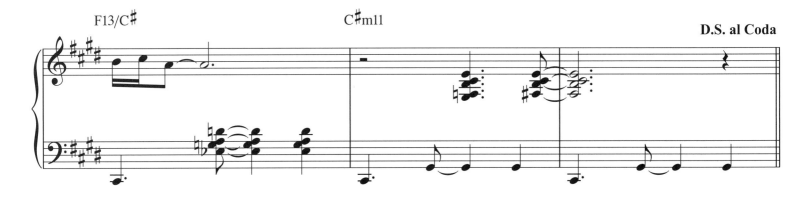

CODA

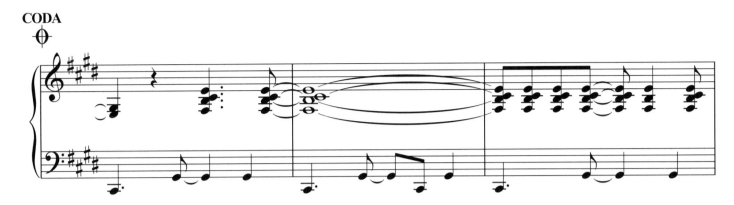

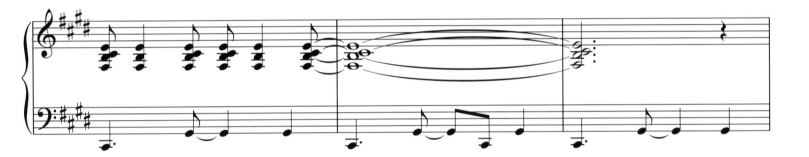

SEÑOR BLUES

Words and Music by
HORACE SILVER

Moderate Latin

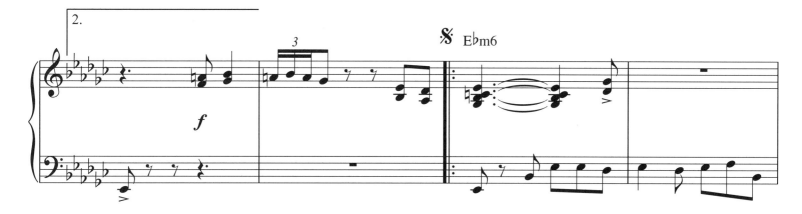

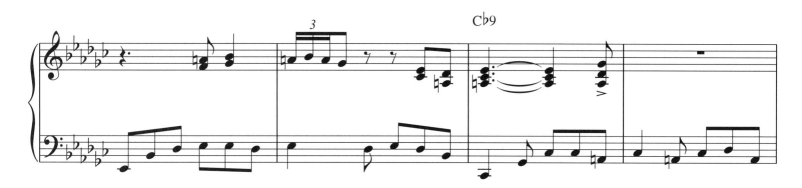

70

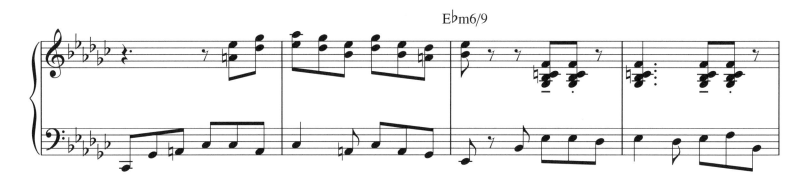

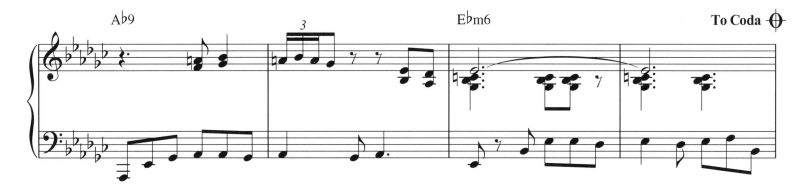

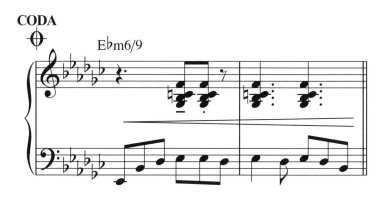

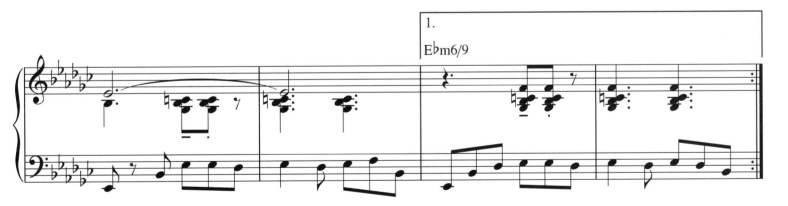

SIGHIN' AND CRYIN'

Words and Music by
HORACE SILVER

Moderately slow Swing

(L.H. alone first time)

Arrangement based on one by Horace Silver

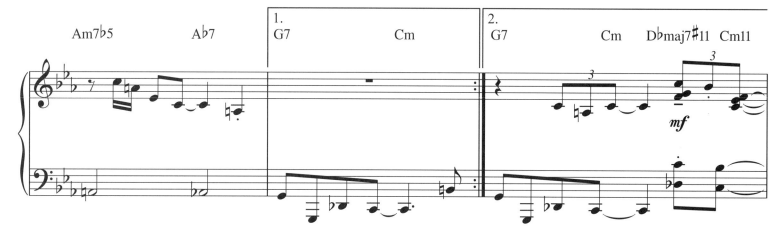

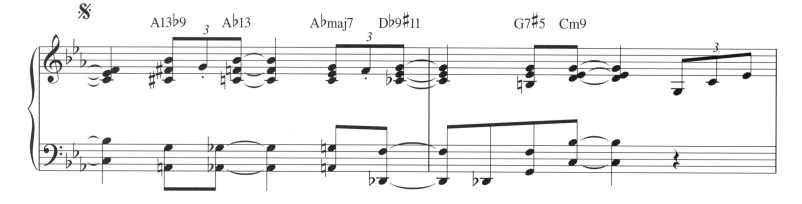

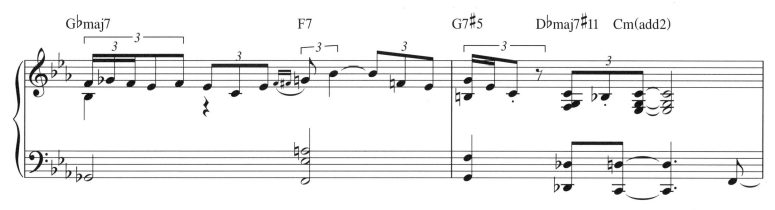

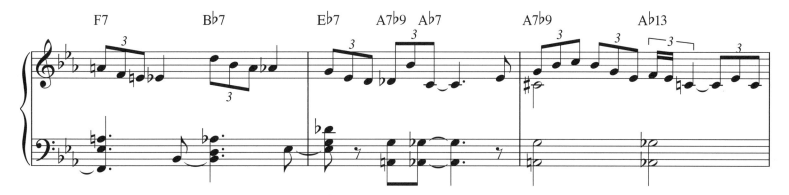

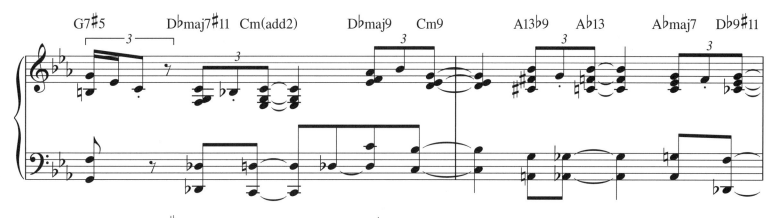

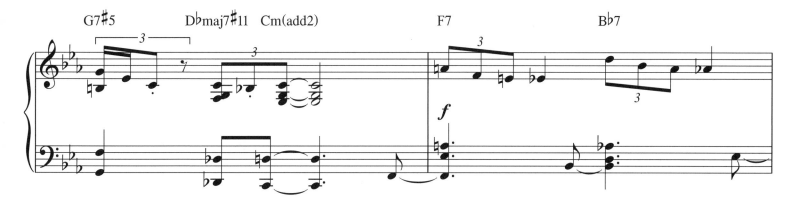

74

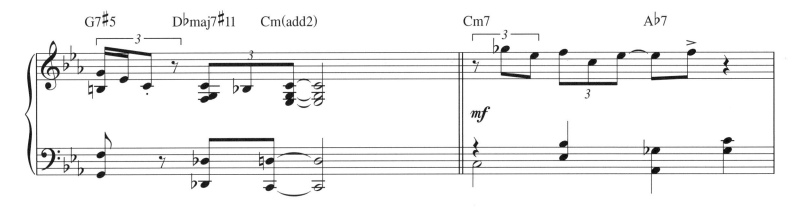

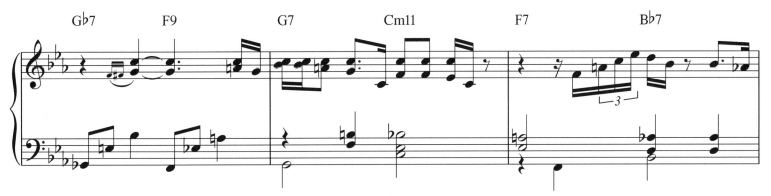

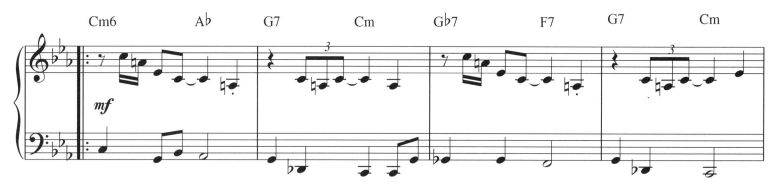

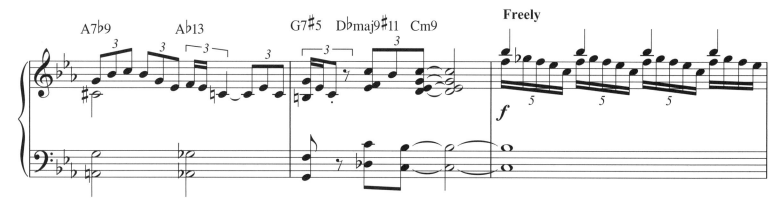

SISTER SADIE

Words and Music by
HORACE SILVER

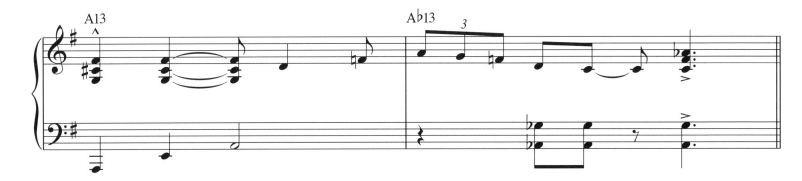

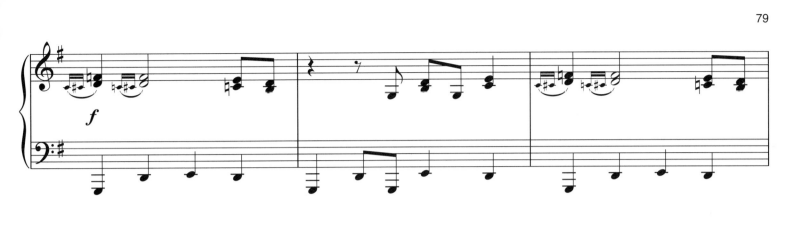

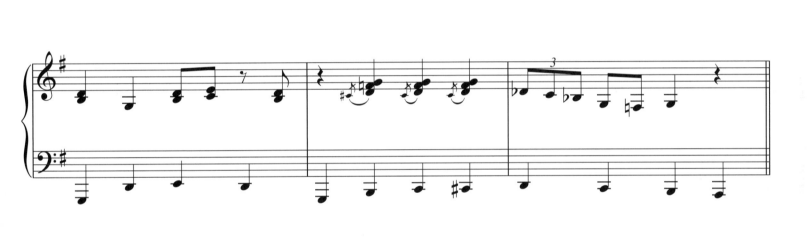

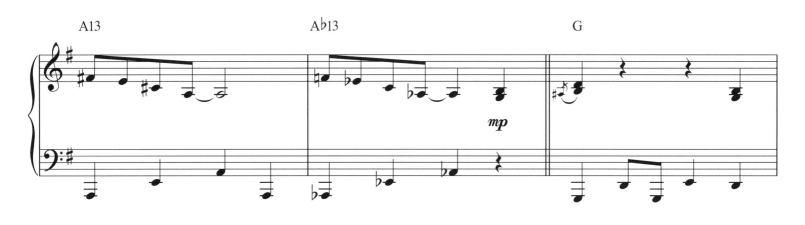

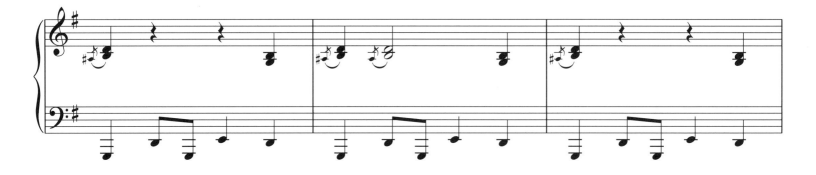

D.S. al Coda

CODA

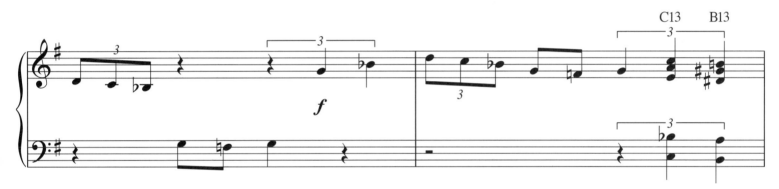

SONG FOR MY FATHER

Words and Music by
HORACE SILVER

Moderate Latin groove

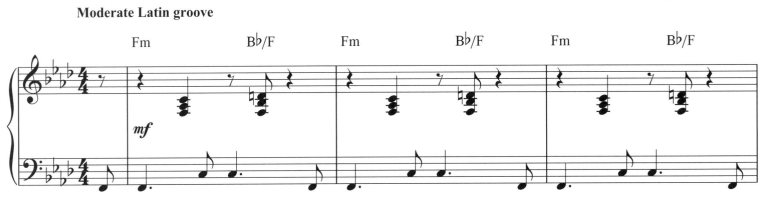

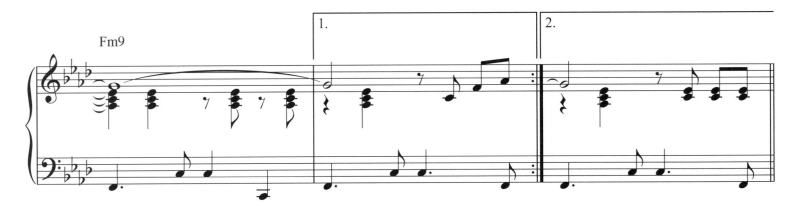

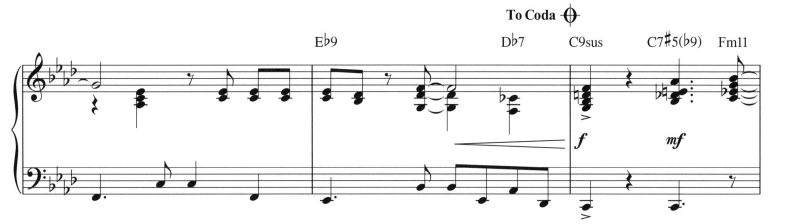

To Coda

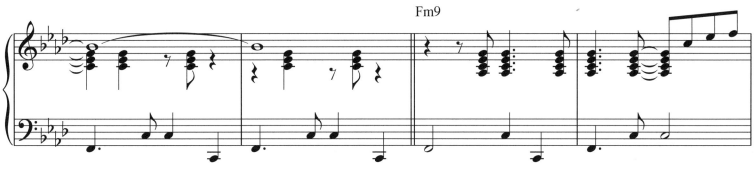

Solo based on one by Horace Silver

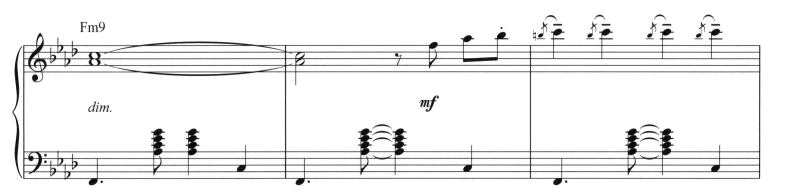

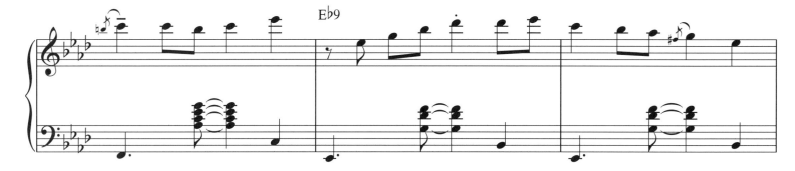

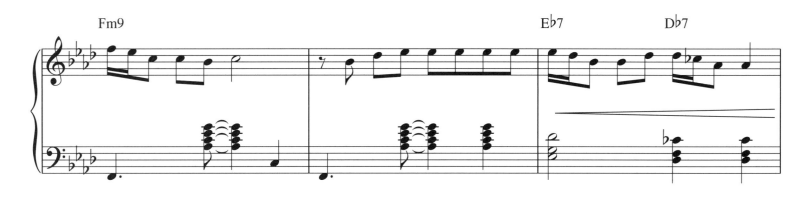

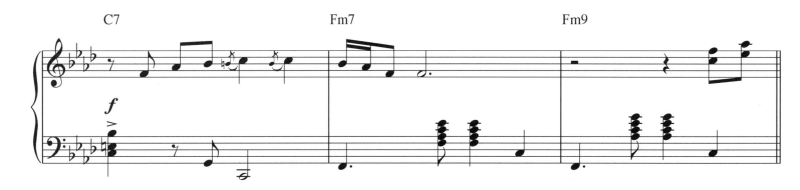

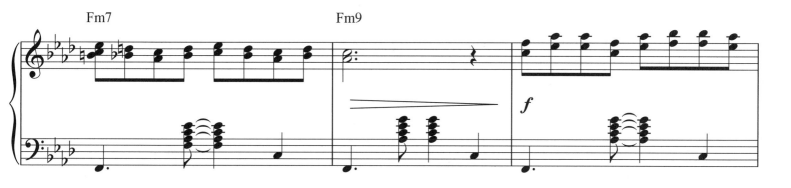

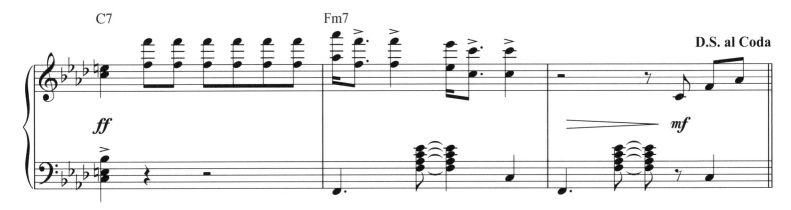

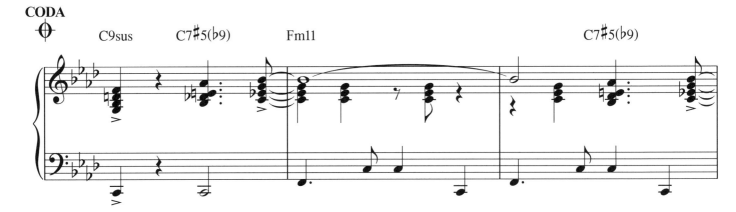

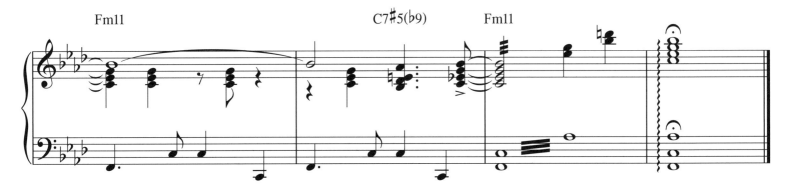

THOU SWELL
from A CONNECTICUT YANKEE

Words by LORENZ HART
Music by RICHARD RODGERS

Bright Swing

Arrangement based on one by Horace Silver

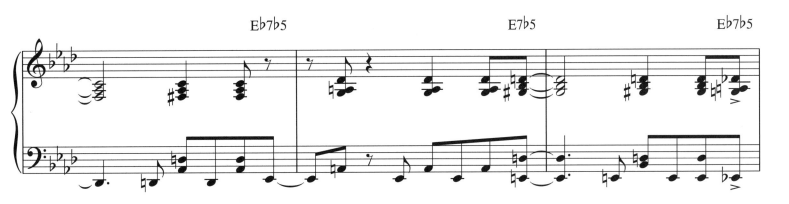

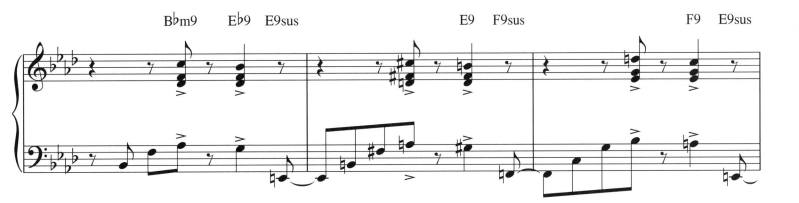

88

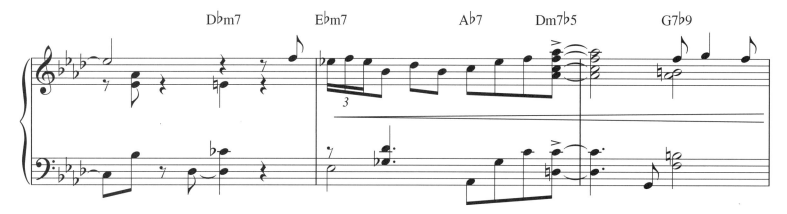

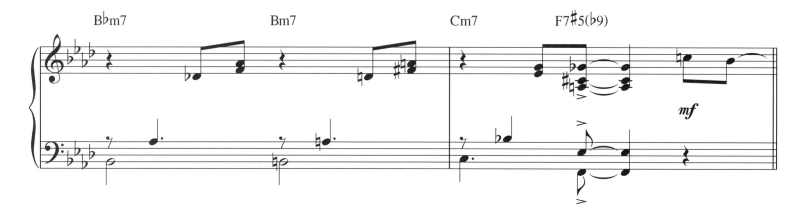

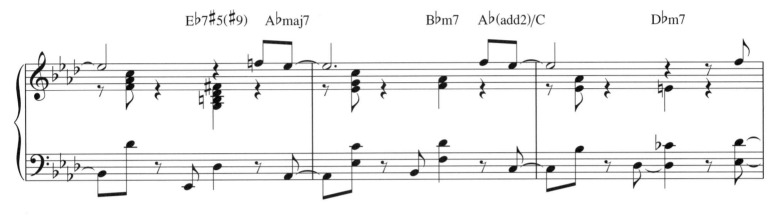

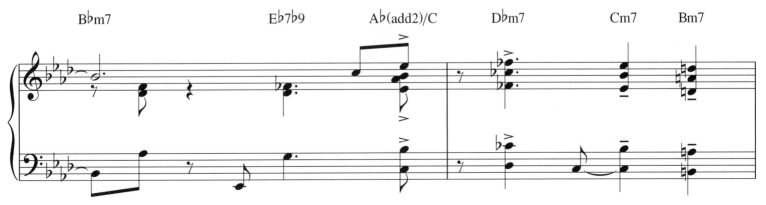

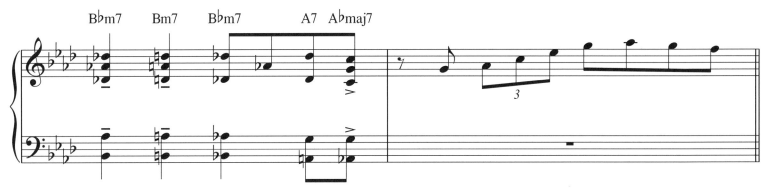

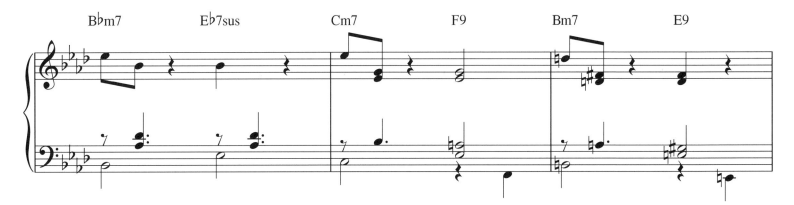

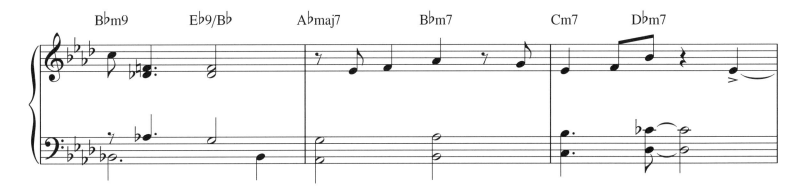

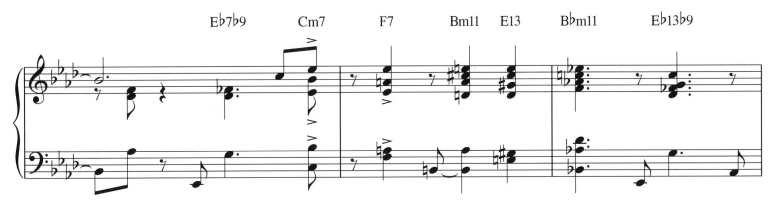

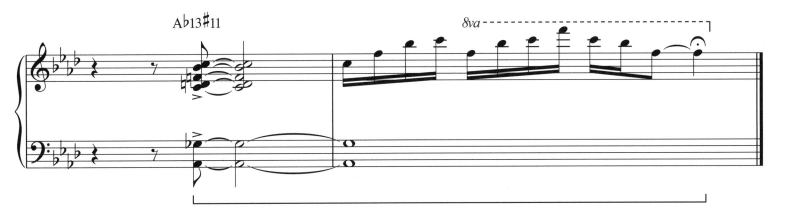

THE TOKYO BLUES

Words and Music by
HORACE SILVER

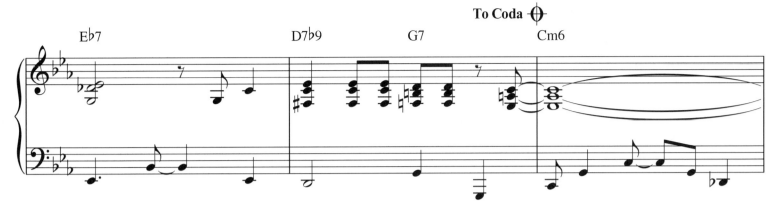

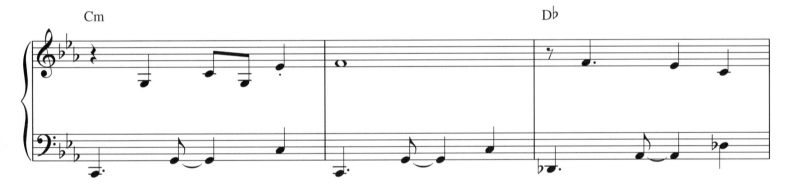

Solo based on one by Horace Silver

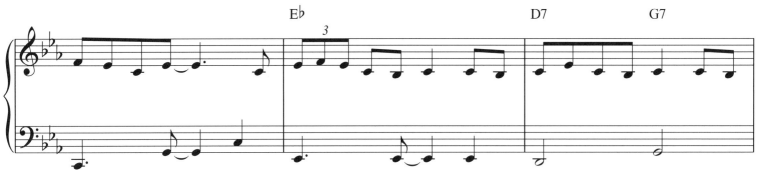

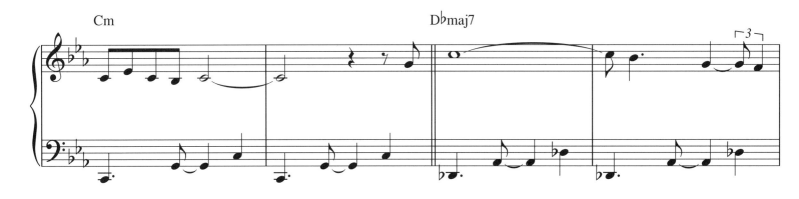

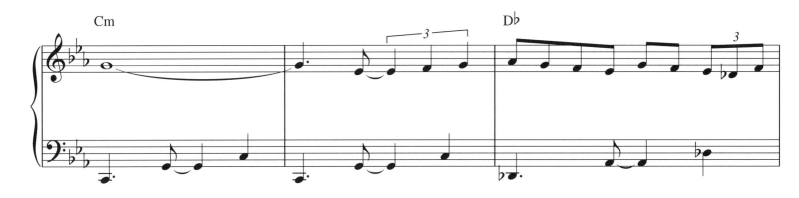

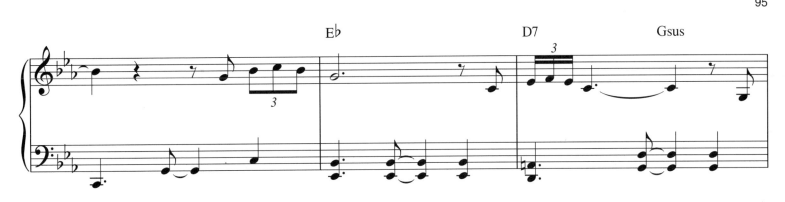

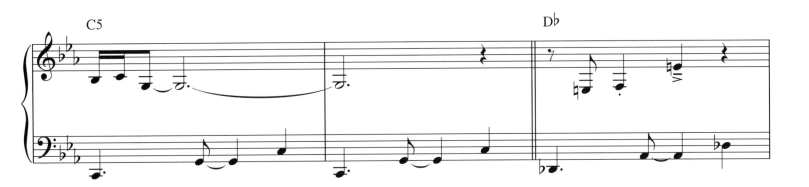

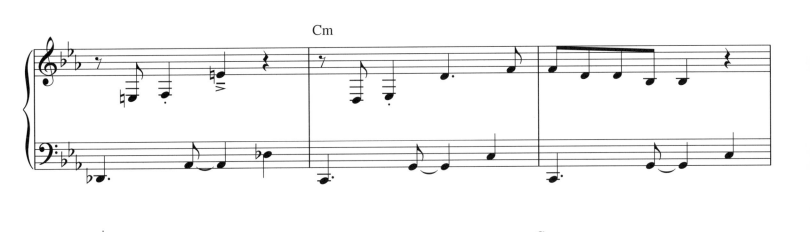

96

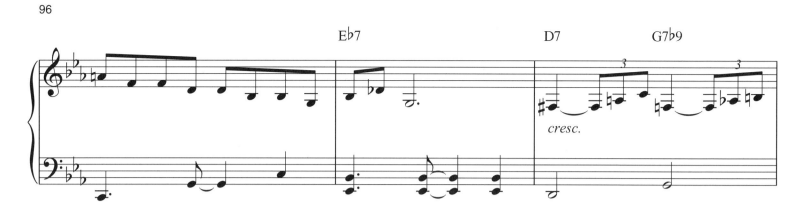

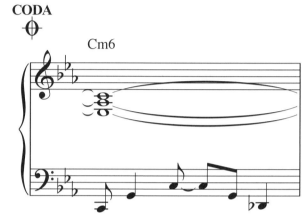